Little Bunny Had A Secret

By Debbie Joski Schmidt
Illustrations by Krista Schmidt

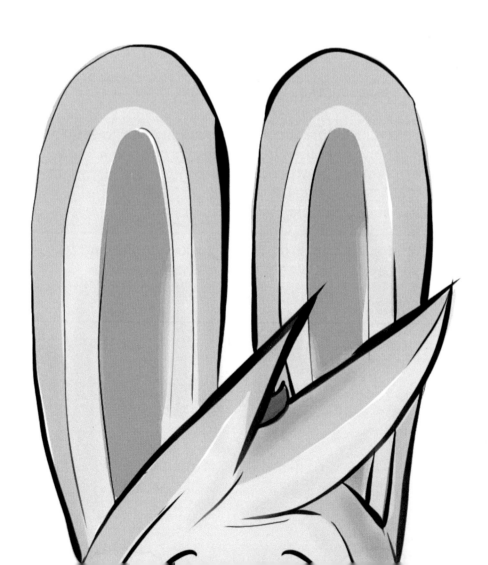

© 2020 Debbie Joski Schmidt

All rights reserved. No portion of this book may be reproduced, stored in a retrieval system or transmitted in any form or by any means – electronic, mechanical, photocopy, recording, scanning or other except for brief quotations in critical reviews or articles, without the prior written permission of Debbie Joski Schmidt.

"Little Bunny" is a trademark of Debbie Joski Schmidt and Invested Stories, LLC in the United States and/or other countries.

ISBN 10 is 0-9986240-2-0
ISBN 13 is 978-0-9986240-2-0

This book is dedicated to the two talented ladies in my life that made this story come alive: my daughter-in-law, Krista Schmidt, for the creative and fun illustrations; and my daughter, Cara Schmidt, for an inviting and colorful design and layout.

And for editing assistance, a big thank you to Barbara Simms and Sandra Judd.

Little Bunny Had A Secret
By Debbie Joski Schmidt
Illustrations by Krista Schmidt

Little Bunny had a secret. He didn't know who to tell first.

"I've got a secret," he told a grandma at the bus stop.

"That's nice, dearie," she said.

The grandma was too busy waiting for the bus to listen to Little Bunny's secret.

She patted his head before he hopped away.

He saw Mrs. Jones, his schoolteacher, leaving the grocery store.

Maybe she'd like to know my secret, he thought.

He quickly hopped over to tell her the secret.

But he wasn't paying attention and hopped onto the wet cement with the sign next to it that said, "Do not hop on."

A big, tall bunny pulled Little Bunny out of the cement. "Now be careful," he said sternly to the little bunny.

"I promise," Little Bunny said, shaking the cement off his foot.

But when the big, tall bunny set Little Bunny down,
Mrs. Jones was gone. Little Bunny hopped away.

His ears perked up when he saw his friend Raphael coming out of the bookstore across the street.

"Oh, I bet he'd like to know my secret!" Little Bunny said.

But Little Bunny had to cross the street first.

He waited with the other bunnies at the light. By the time he got to the other side, his friend was gone.

Little Bunny didn't see anyone else to tell, so he decided to hop home.

"Maybe I'll see someone on the way," he thought.

"Hi Little Bunny," his friend Elizabeth yelled out a car window.

Little Bunny waved.

He wondered if Elizabeth would like to know the secret, but the car drove right by.

"Oh well," Little Bunny said.

He kept hopping.

"It's not every day a little bunny has a secret to share," he said out loud to himself on his way home. "I know someone will want to hear it."

He heard a tiny voice.

"I would like to hear your secret," the voice said.

Little Bunny stopped.

"Is that you, Raphael? Or is that you, Elizabeth?" he said, wondering where the voice was coming from.

He looked over his right shoulder and then his left.

He looked up and then down and then spun around to look behind him.

No one was next to him, under him, or even behind him.

I must be dreaming, he thought.

He started hopping home again, but faster this time, just in case the tiny voice came back.

"Woohoo, you hop fast Little Bunny!" the tiny voice said.

Little Bunny put on his bunny foot brakes, stopping as fast as he could.

"Who are you?" Little Bunny asked, looking all around. "And where are you?"

He was getting dizzy from turning around and around. But it was also very fun. He started laughing.

The tiny voice started laughing, too.

"Whee, this is fun!" it said.

Then Little Bunny felt the tiniest little tug on the fur between his long ears.

"I'm up here, silly bunny," the tiny voice said.

Little Bunny had an idea.

"I can spin even faster in the meadow. I'll show you," he said to the something holding onto his fur. "But hold on!"

Little Bunny hopped to the meadow as fast as he could, then spun around and around so many times that he fell over.

"That was fun," the tiny voice said. "I've never gotten that dizzy or spun that fast in my whole life!"

Before Little Bunny could answer, Elizabeth and Raphael came hopping over.

"Hey," they said, "that looks like fun. Can we play with you?"

"Yes," Little Bunny said. The bunnies played and played. Soon other bunnies joined them.

The meadow was full of bunnies. Bunnies ran and skipped, rolled and danced, and played hide and seek and tag, and when they were too tired to do anything else, they just laid on the grass to watch the clouds.

Little Bunny had a lot of fun, more fun than he ever imagined. He had so much fun that he even forgot he had a secret.

When it was five o'clock, the bunnies had to go home.

"See you tomorrow!" they yelled to one another.

Little Bunny hopped home.

He thought about all the bunnies playing in the meadow.

He smiled and said to himself, "I had a lot of fun."

"I did too," he heard.

"You're still up there?" Little Bunny asked.

"Yes," he heard. "It was fun with all of your friends."

Little Bunny said, "I am lucky to have so many friends. Are you my friend?"

"I am," the tiny voice answered.

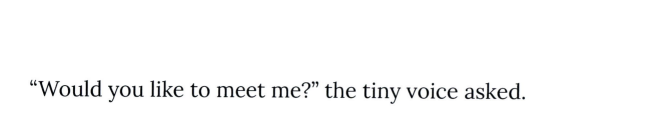

"Would you like to meet me?" the tiny voice asked.

"I would," Little Bunny answered.

"Hold out your foot. But don't be scared," the voice said.

Little Bunny was puzzled.

"Why would I be scared of a tiny voice?" he asked.

"You'll see," the voice said.

Little Bunny held out his front foot.

Suddenly a dark purple rhinoceros bug with an extra-long horn and dark wings landed on his toe.

He almost shook the ugly bug off. Then he remembered.

The purple rhinoceros bug waved a tiny hand and said, in her tiny voice, "Nice to meet you, Little Bunny! Are you surprised?"

Little Bunny nodded and said, "I am surprised. But it's nice to meet you, too, purple rhinoceros bug, however you look. What's your name?"

"My name is Cornelia. It was my grandmother's name. Do you like it?" she wondered. She did a little dance on his foot.

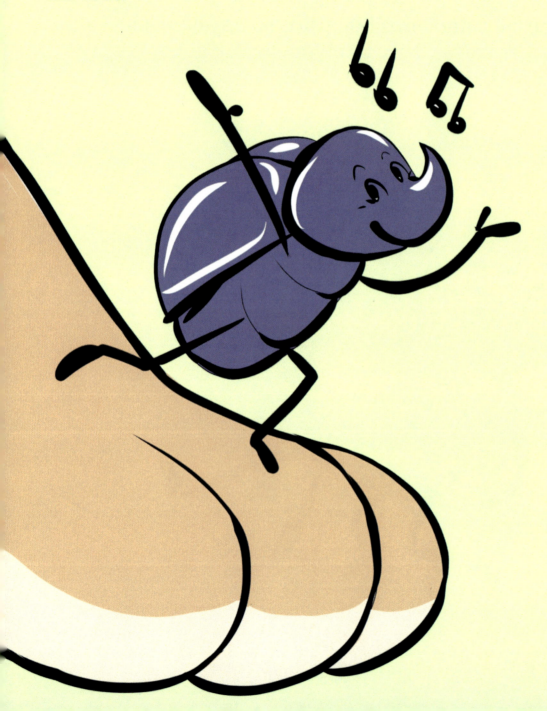

Little Bunny nodded. "I like your name and I like your dance too."

"Thank you," Cornelia said. She opened her wings and looked like she was going to fly away.

"Hey, do you want to go for another ride, this time to my house up over there?"

He pointed to the blue house on the hill.

"Yes," Cornelia the purple rhinoceros bug said.

She held onto Little Bunny's fur between his ears and laughed and laughed the whole way to his house on the hill.

"That was fun!" they said when they got there.

The front door opened. It was Little Bunny's mama.

She said, "Little Bunny, we're having a special dinner tonight. Come get ready."

Before he went inside, Cornelia the purple rhinoceros bug said, "Wait!"

She landed on his foot again.

"What is it?" Little Bunny wanted to know.

"I am wondering," Cornelia said slowly, "what your secret is."

"Oh, my secret," Little Bunny giggled. "You would like to know what my secret is?"

"I would," she said excitedly.

"Well, my secret is that today is my birthday!" Little Bunny said.

"Happy birthday, Little Bunny! I'm glad I got to meet you on your birthday." She gave his neck a hug and said, "And I'm glad you're my friend."

She did a pretty dance in the air before she flew away.

"Come visit me soon," Little Bunny yelled after her.

She flew back and said, in her tiny voice, "I will. See you soon, little birthday bunny!"

He waved good-bye to his new friend.

Little Bunny smiled all the way through his big birthday dinner and birthday presents.

He even smiled during bath time and when his mama was tucking him in. She leaned over and kissed him on the forehead.

He said, "This was my best birthday ever."

Before he closed his eyes, he said, "Mama, I have a secret!"

Mama, I have a secret!

The End

Check out Brownie Mouse
by Debbie Joski Schmidt!

Other books by Debbie Joski Schmidt

The Adventures of Brownie Mouse series

The Adventures of Brownie Mouse: Story One: Brownie's Brownie Shop

No one really notices that Brownie Mouse™ has moved to Mouseville. That is, until delicious smells begin floating through the town. Everyone is sniffing the air and asking each other, "What is that delicious smell and where is it coming from?" The school children, the neighbors, the firemice, and even the Mayor all want to know!

Come along on the sweetest adventure Mouseville has ever experienced and be part of the search for who is behind the wonderful cheesy chocolate smell. Join in "The Adventures of Brownie Mouse"!

As we learn from Brownie Mouse, baking can be fun and exciting! So, as a special treat, you'll find a Brownie's Brownie recipe to try at the end of the story.

The Adventures of Brownie Mouse: Story Two: The Really Delicious Brownie Ideas

All of Mouseville loves Brownie Mouse's famous brownies. But now, he's fresh out of ideas for new brownie flavors! After a mysterious break-in, Brownie gets some interesting ideas from some unexpected places.

But will they be enough to keep his spot as the Best Brownie Baker in all of Mouseville? Make your own batch of chocolatey goodness along with Brownie and his friends as he bakes his way through another fun adventure.

Both are currently available on Amazon!

About the Author

Debbie Joski Schmidt has been a storyteller since her children were small. After putting the stories to paper, she found she enjoyed writing stories as telling them. She enjoys simple story lines with cute and happy characters with a bit of nostalgia thrown in. In her full time work, she is a wellness coach dietitian, and enjoys baking, spending time with her family of six, and cat family of five.

About the Illustrator

Krista Schmidt dabbles in colorful illustrations as a hobby. She can seamlessly create so much joy and fun in a single illustration! She is so good at what she does both on the computer and in her work as an x-ray technician. She is the author's daughter-in-law and has a love for all things in nature ... animals, reptiles, bugs, birds, etc. of all shapes and sizes.